I0113215

FUNNY BUGS

Funny Bugs

Rosemary Butler

Sun on Earth™ Books
Heathsville, Virginia

Published by Sun on Earth™ Books

www.sunonearth.com

Copyright © 2021 by Rosemary Butler

All rights reserved under International and Pan-American Copyright Conventions. No part of this book may be reproduced or transmitted in any manner whatsoever without written permission from the publisher, except in the case of brief quotations embodied in critical articles or reviews.

Illustrations by the author.

Publisher's Cataloging-in-Publication Data
Butler, Rosemary.
    Funny bugs / Rosemary Butler.— 1st ed.
        p. cm.
    ISBN: 978-1-883378-14-1
            1. Insects—Poetry.
            I. Title.

    PS309.F7 .B88 .F8669 2021
    811'.6—dc23

Library of Congress Control Number: 2021933315

ISBN: 978-1-883378-14-1

Some bugs are nasty.

Some bugs are sweet.

But don't let them crawl

On your fingers or feet.

Please turn the page.

Then feast your eyes.

Here come FUNNY BUGS –

What a silly surprise!

— Rosemary Butler

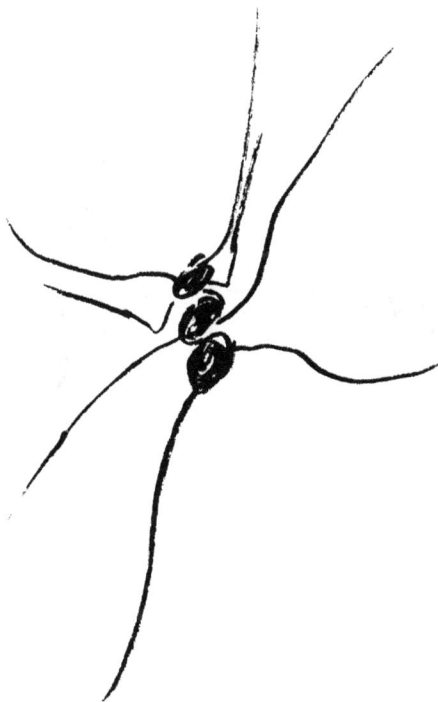

The Abracadabra Ant

The abracadabra charmed ant

To stop speaking in nonsense — he'll grant

That he'll try — yes, he guesses,

And simply confesses,

"To quit speaking in nonsense, I CAN'T."

An Ant

Ants all like to travel.

Their favorite place to go:

Is where there's lots of ice

And also lots of snow.

You'll note

Their vote

is

ANTARCTICA

Another Ant

With antipathy toward the ant,

I refuse to compose an anthem.

    The birds and bees

    I try to please,

But ants, I just can't stand them.

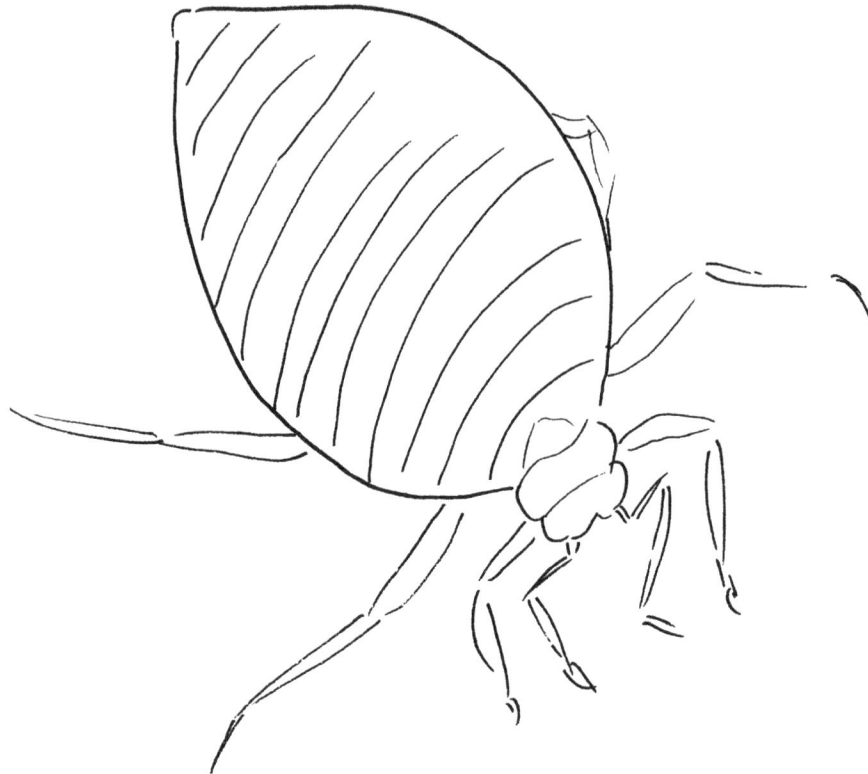

Bed Bug

A bedbug's favorite place to hide

Is in a warm and cozy bed,

In a mattress or its rounded edge,

Or even under a costly spread.

To find new beds he'll take a ride

On pets or clothes. He has no pride.

Here comes the bedbug stealthily creeping

And finds an innocent person sleeping.

He BITES. The sleeper's unaware

That bedbugs simply DO NOT CARE.

Bob Bug

You forgot the time!

You're in a mixed-up state.

So who's to blame?

The bug called "discomBOBulate."

He's always near you.

He thinks you're great.

When you're confused,

Blame it on your bug friend,

"discomBOBulate."

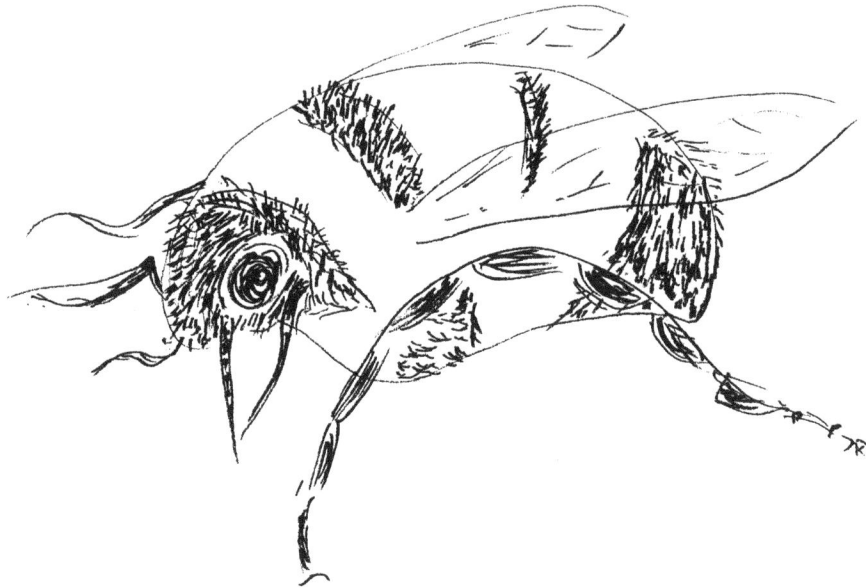

Bumblebee

Beware of the humble Bumblebee,

In his black and yellow suit.

He's a very rough and tumble bee.

The girl bees call him cute.

Bush Fly

The bush fly hangs out everywhere
In all parts of Australia.
He loves to go to drunken feasts —
To buggy bacchanalia.

The Carpenter Ant

The busybody carpenter ant

Is building a house

Or planting a plant.

No stopping him

In any way,

Just let him build

And plant all day.

I think he will eventually use

The world's supply of nails and screws.

This ant collects all kinds of seeds,

And does not know that most are weeds.

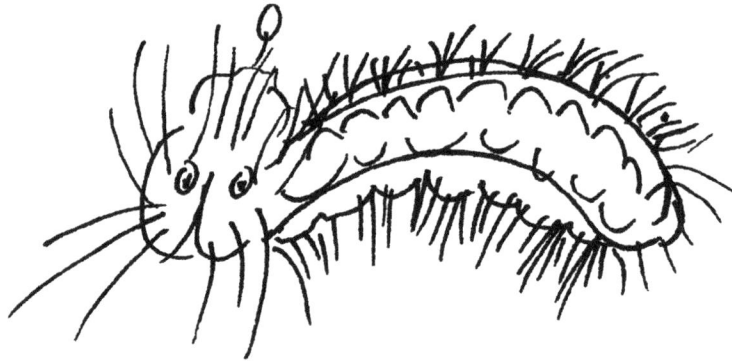

caterpillar

The fat and fuzzy caterpillar

Would like to write a scary thriller.

His friends inform him, "You can't write.

You might as well go fly a kite!"

Chinch Bug

The chinch bug has a tiny chin,

And has an awful bite.

He may not ever bite you,

But then again he might.

The Cicada

Male cicadas make a noise:

A rowdy buzz like boisterous boys.

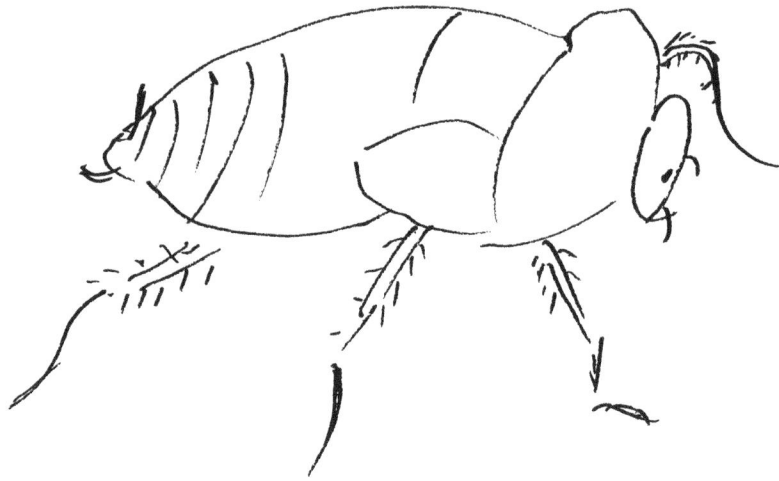

COCKROACH

The cockroach has an angry face.

We know he knows he knows his place.

The cockroach at his very best,

Is always a domestic pest.

A Cricket

Would you really buy a ticket

To see a crazy, dancing cricket?

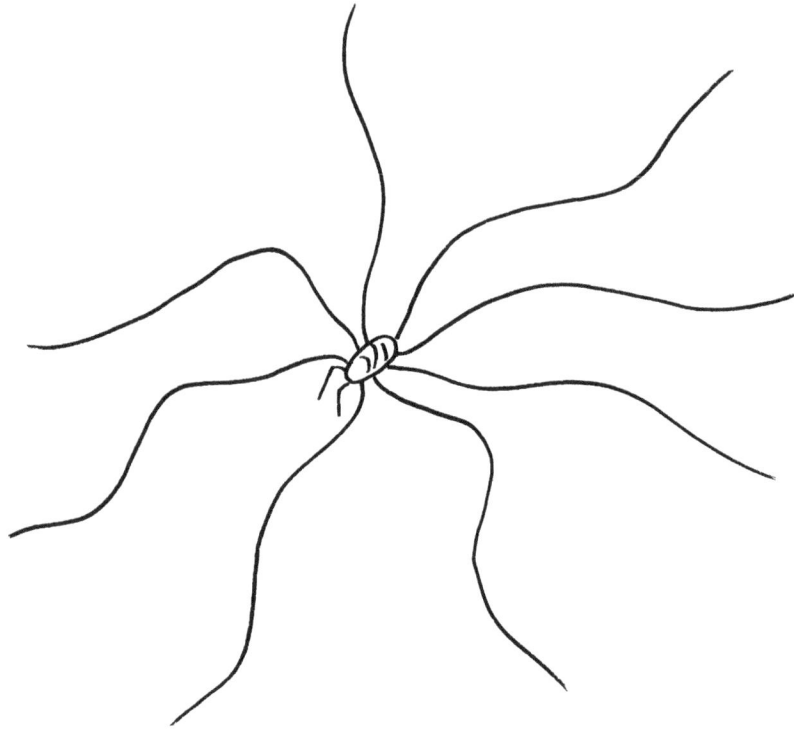

Daddy Long-legs

Daddy Long-legs legs are thin.

Perfect for playing a mandolin,

Plus a violin,

And a big bass drum.

To this concert

I'm sure nobody will come.

Damselfly

A damselfly is like a Lorelei,

Except she never sings;

And when she takes a rest,

She likes to close her wings.

DEMOISELLE

In ranking bugs, the noblest bug

Must be the Demoiselle.

In bugdom's hierarchy,

She's the Coco (bug) Chanel.

Dragonfly

Why would a dragonfly want to fly?
I guess we'll just have to ask him why.

Dragonflies will hover
Above a stream or pond.
If they're disturbed,
They'll fly straight up
To treetops or beyond.

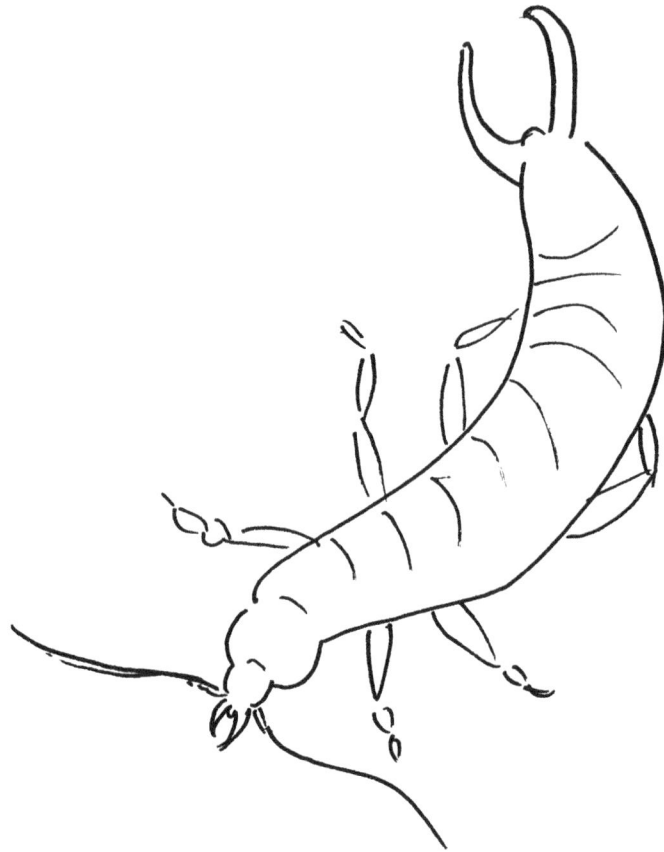

The Earwig

Did you ever hear

Why an ear needs a wig?

Unless it's the ear

Of a baldheaded pig.

Fire Ant

Ants are simply nonessential,

Since they are mainly pestilential.

A sign to hang on every tree,

For all who hire ants to see:

FIRE ANTS!

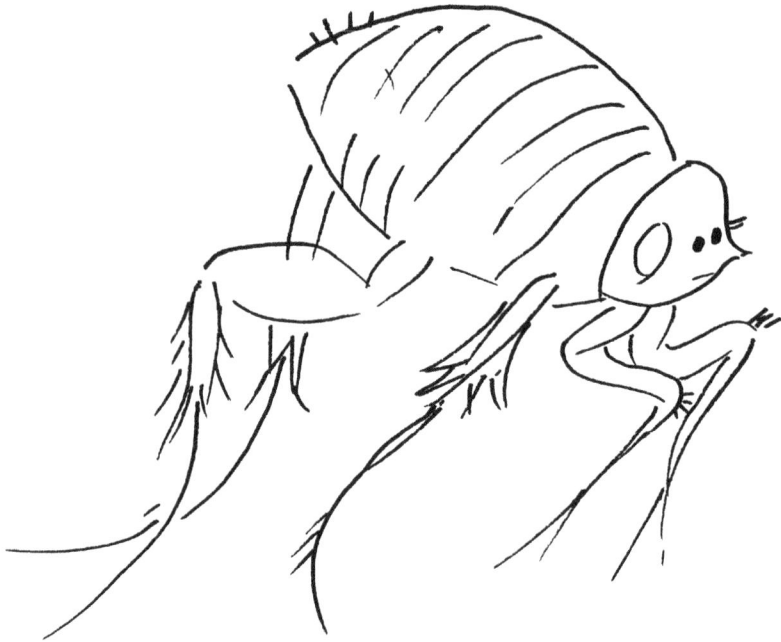

Flea

If you see

A flea,

Flee!

Take flight

Or he'll bite!

Glowworm

The glowworm is a very slow worm,

Who likes to live in damp, dark caves.

He wants to glow to let you know

He's glad you came to say "hello."

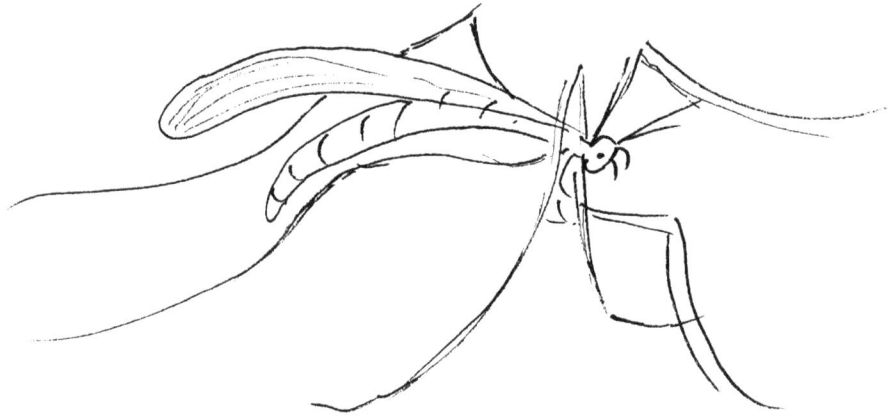

Gnat

A verse about obnoxious gnats:

Their offspring are annoying brats.

Shunned by every man and beast,

From North and South and West and East.

I wish to make a modest jest:

All gnats are quite gnattily dressed.

Observe the gnice, but gnaughty gnat.

He's gneither thin, nor gnever fat.

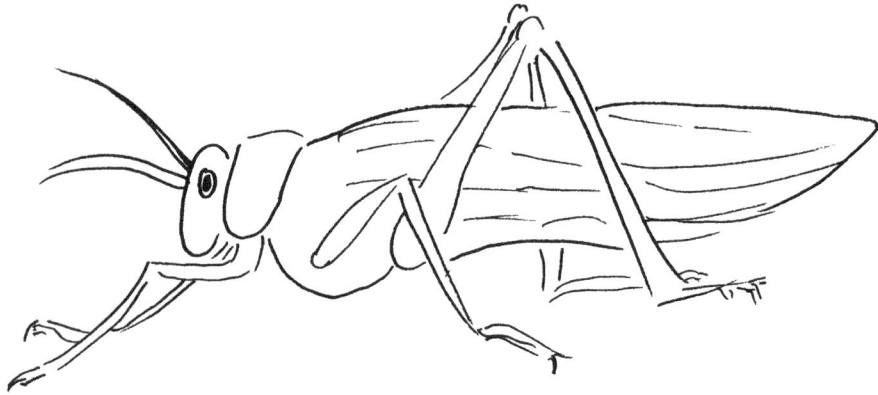

The Grasshopper

Grasshoppers really like to hop.

They seem to never want to stop.

Why do they always like to jump?

I think they must have Restless Rump.

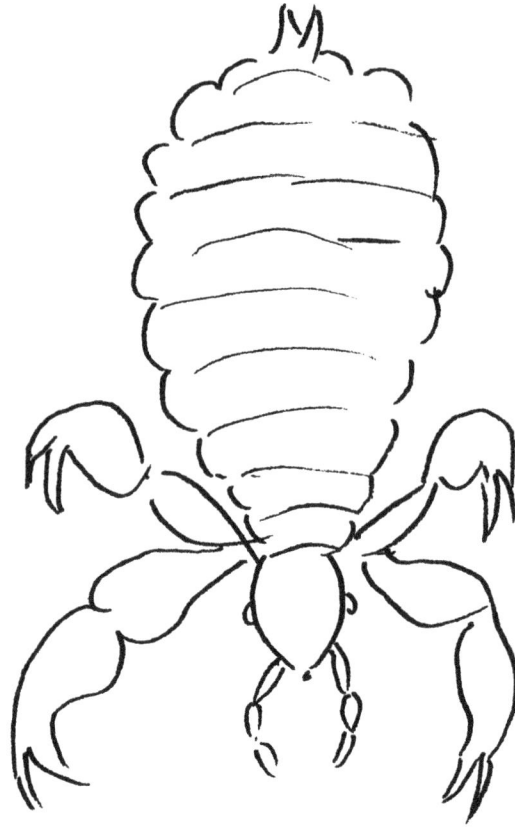

Head Louse

Have you ever heard of

The dastardly head louse?

He's outlawed from entering

Your house or my house.

His cousins are called by the

Short name of "lice,"

Which compared with "louse,"

sounds really quite nice!

Honey Bee

I would like to invite a polite honeybee

To come to my house for a nice cup of tea.

I'll make the tea and provide buttered toast.

She'll bring the honey,

For which she may boast

That she made it herself,

That's what honeybees do.

How I'll manage this party, I haven't a clue!

Hornet

The only occasion

I'd call Murder Hornet,

Is when neighbor's teen

Starts to practice his cornet.

House Fly

The house fly always flies

In search of a tiny pool,

Especially one of cocktail size,

To plunge in vodkas, rums, and ryes.

Swimming around and around he tries

To find where buried treasure lies,

Until he finally sinks and dies —

A grave both 80 proof and cool.

June Bug

June Bugs are often seen in June.

So maybe they're on their honeymoon.

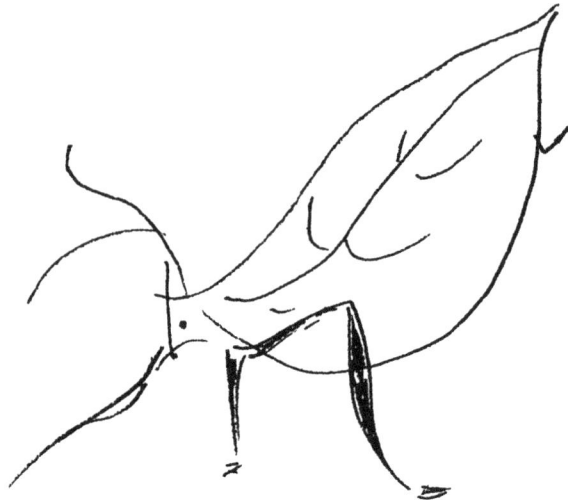

Katydid

The Katydid bug

Just calls out her name:

"Katydid! Katydid!"

All the words are the same.

Katydid! Katydid! Katydid!

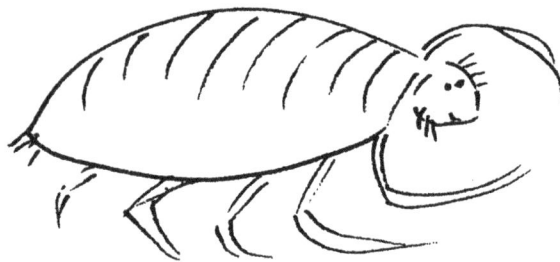

The Kindness Bug

Here comes

The Kindness Bug.

She gives you a bite,

But also a hug.

Ladybug

Ladybugs like to be

Properly dressed.

In their polka-dot coats.

Everyone is impressed.

Leaf Insect

This bug likes to hide

In the leaves on a branch.

To find him at all,

No one has a chance.

To look like a leaf

Is his perfect disguise.

To find this sly bug,

No one even tries.

Lightning Bug

Tell me, did you ever wonder,

If lightning bugs like storms with thunder?

The Locust

Mr. Locust, how do you feel?

"Hungry, I missed my midday meal—

Of plants that are fresh

From the fields and green.

I call them my favorite Green Cuisine."

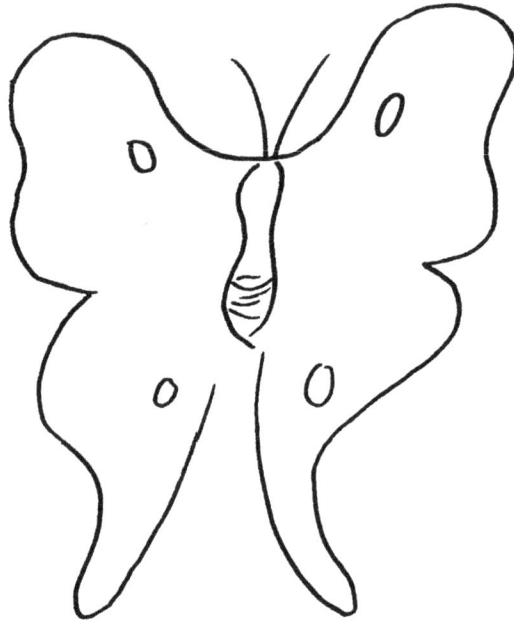

Luna Moth and Tick

Here's a thing that I don't want to hear:

A luna moth dating a tick.

Her wings are soft green

And transparently sheer.

His body looks like an old brick.

All at once, luna moth starts to think,

"Myself, I am ready to kick!

A disaster my dating that insect!

Linked together, we'd be called 'LUNA-TIC.'"

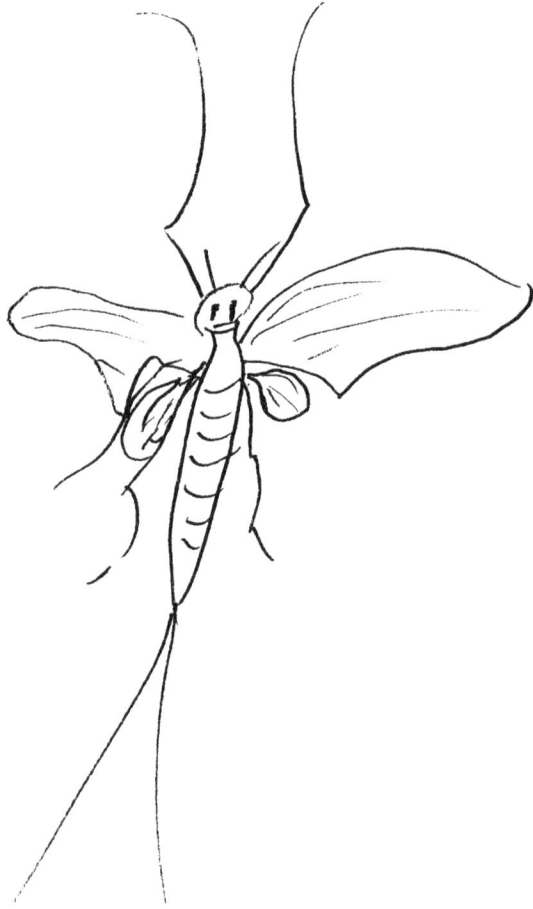

Mayfly

The mayfly may fly away
On just two pairs of wings.
Flying hither and thither
Like daring ding-a-lings.

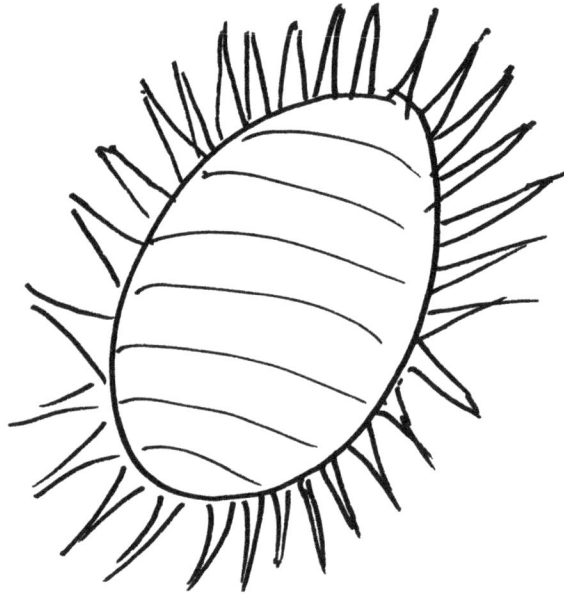

Mealybug

What is a mealybug's favorite meal?

Whatever is served must have great eye appeal.

He especially likes generous helpings of veal,

Served with pink mashed potatoes and

Shaved lemon peel.

Next, should be something all sticky and sweet,

Which mealybugs always find yummy to eat.

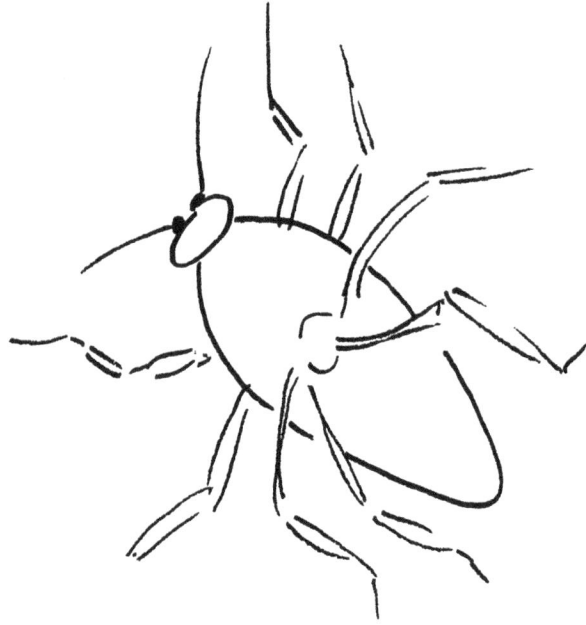

Midge

Where do you think

You will find a midge?

Up on a ridge?

Crossing a bridge?

Since this midge is often

Afraid of high heights,

He'll not go there at all

On dark, stormy nights.

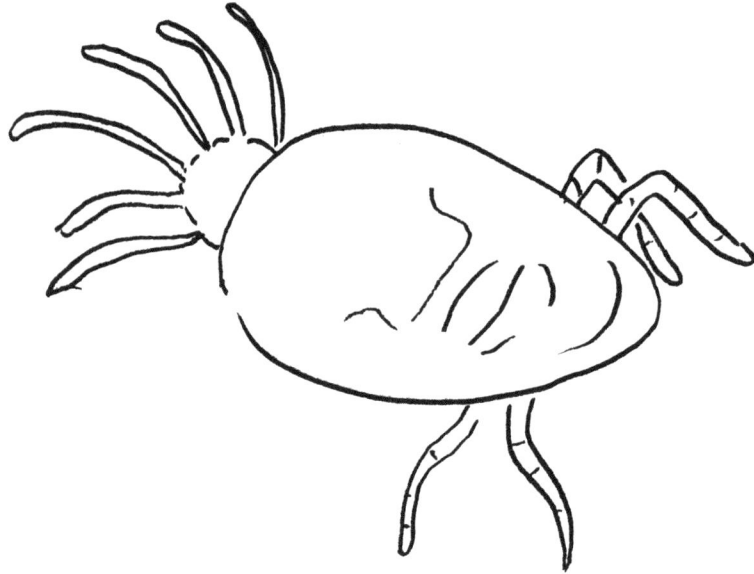

THE MITE

The madly mysterious mite—

Too small to be seen

In the day

Or the night.

He's simply so very terribly small,

That maybe you won't even see him at all.

But you might!

Midge

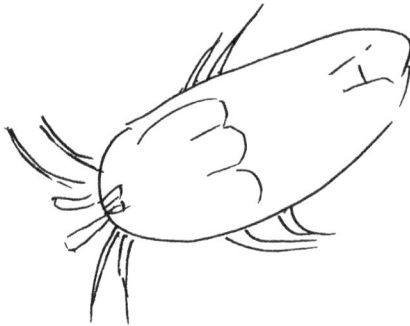

Mite

Tell me the difference:
A midge and a mite?

A mite is a morsel you butter and bite.

A midge is a leftover found in the fridge.

No, no!

A midge is a fly with a couple of wings.
A mite is a chigger, I think never sings.

Each midge and each mite
Is an impudent bug.
Both are quite sassy, sardonic, and smug.

Monarch Butterfly

Monarch butterflies take long trips,

But never ever pack.

Their pretty clothes of orange and black

Are always on their back.

Mosquito

Mosquitoes pretend to be sincere,

But the only thing from them you'll hear

Is a constant hum, and then a bite,

From early morning to late at night.

Mosquitoes never ever should sting.

Instead, they ought to learn to sing.

No-see-um

Now I see them.

Now I don't.

Where have all these insects gone?

I promise they will soon be back

To bother you anon.

No-see-ums think it's lots of fun

To fly around your eyes.

They say they only do this

As a no-see-um surprise.

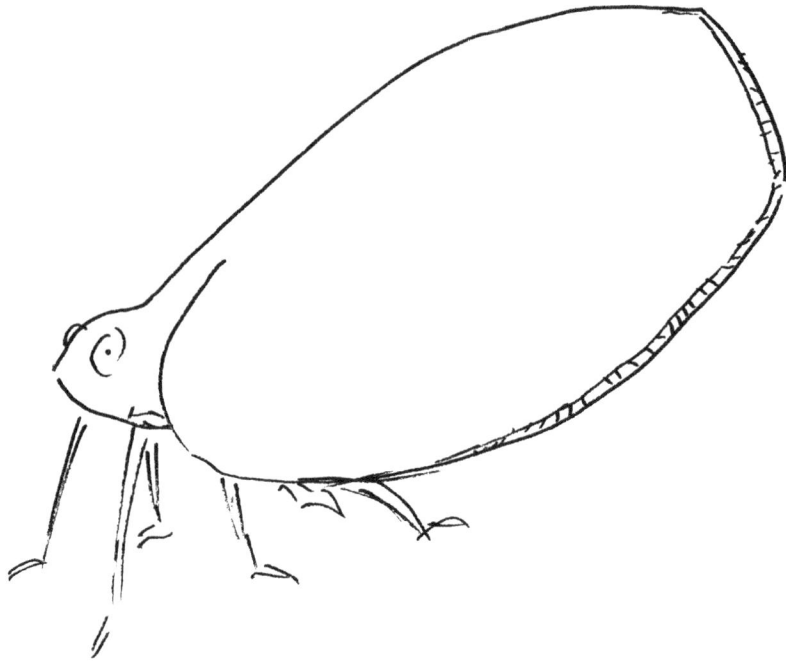

Plant-hopper

The plant hopper looks
Like a six-legged leaf.
It's so realistic,
It's beyond our belief.

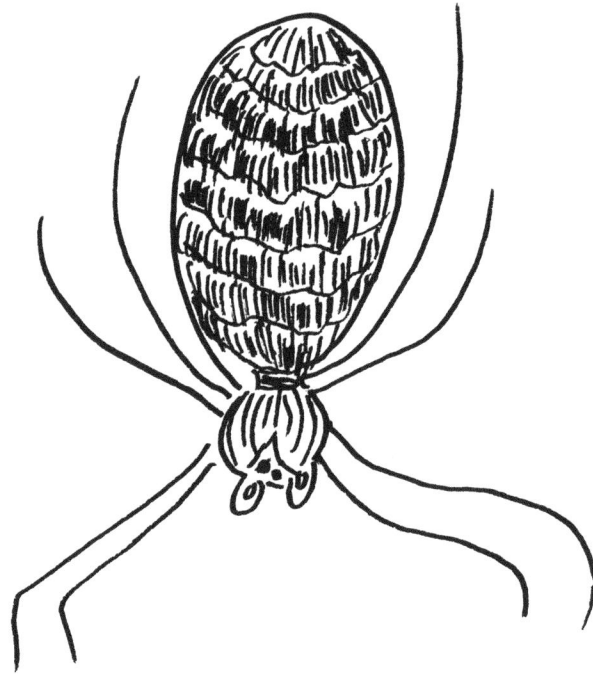

Spider

A spider can weave

A most marvelous web,

Like Charlotte, the Spider.

Then everyone said

Became famous

By author E.B. White.

Charlotte gained fame

From his book overnight,

Charlotte's Web

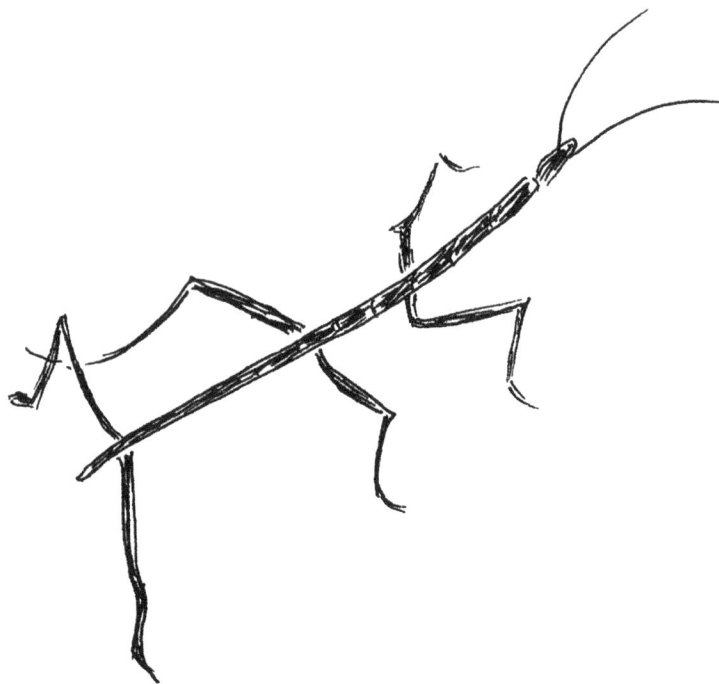

Stick Insect

The stick insect

Is a quick insect,

As speedy as a tick.

A tick belongs

Inside a clock

Since a tick demands a tock.

So what does

A stick insect do?

He'll simply stick around,

Until he finds another stick

And likes what he has found!

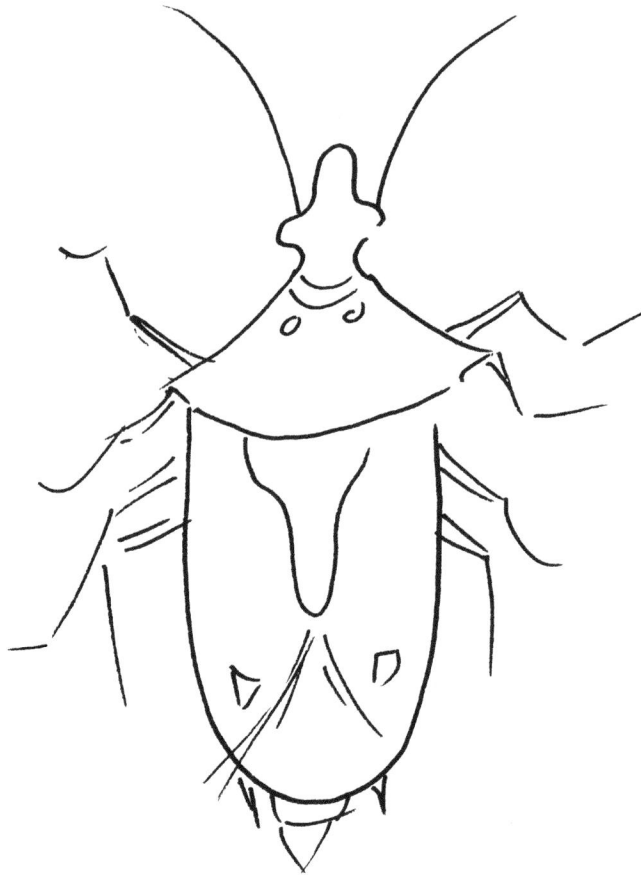

STINK BUG

Beware of this nasty malodorous bug.

He can be hiding under a rug.

You can find him almost anywhere:

In a bed or on a chair.

He does not make a single sound,

Yet he's impossible to be around.

You might find him in the kitchen sink.

You'll know it's this bug, since he has a stink.

His stink is why we always blame him.

STINK BUG is therefore what we name him.

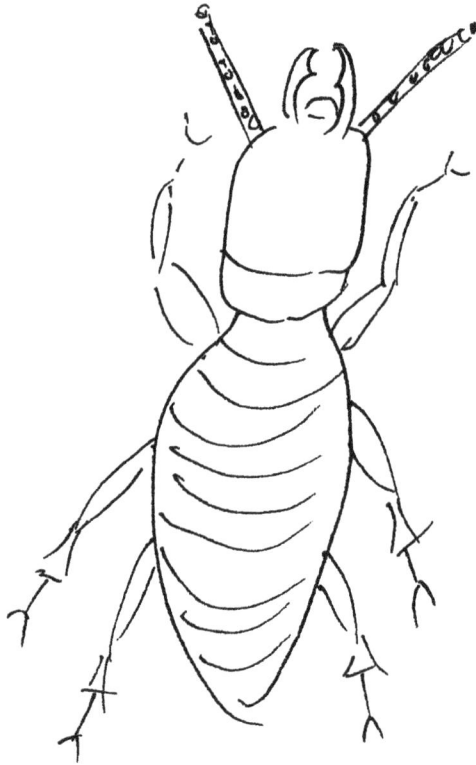

The Termite

An intellectual,

The termite is not.

But he loves books—

He loves them a lot!

At the library door

He likes to greet them.

At the library table,

He likes to eat them.

Thrip

On trips to England
For hungry thrips,
Their favorite food
Is fish and chips.

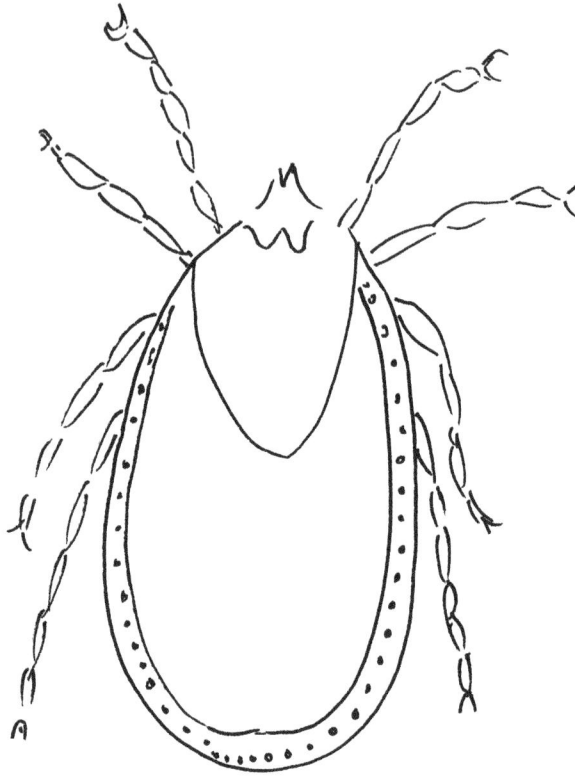

The Tick

Quick, Dick,

Catch that tick,

And send it off

To old St. Nick,

To give to a naughty girl or boy

(much better than a Christmas toy!)

Nick gives the good ones licorice sticks;

To the bad ones only terrible ticks.

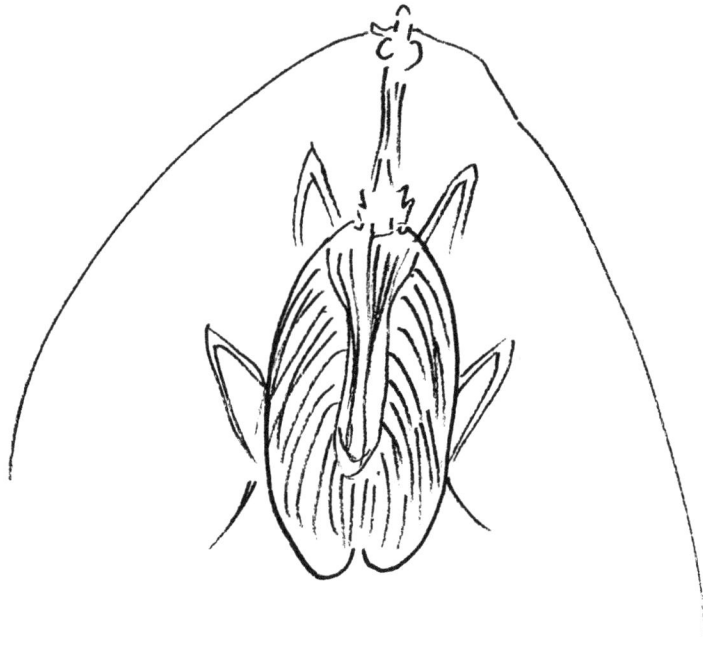

VIOLIN BEETLE

The violin beetle's sweetheart
Told the preacher, "Marry us
And please play at our wedding
Your Stradivarius."

WASP

Here is a problem

You'll have to admit:

You cannot say "wasp,"

Without wanting to spit.

ABOUT THE AUTHOR

Rosemary Butler and Charles, her naval-officer husband, have lived in Spain, the Philippines, and many places in the United States, including Alaska, where she designed the stage sets for the third company of *South Pacific*, which toured Alaska from Fairbanks to the Aleutians in 1951.

In addition to her art, Rosemary has written four books and has illustrated them with her pen and ink drawings. Her first book was *Ghostly Encounters*, a collection of short stories based on her adventures with her husband in England, Ireland, and Spain. Her next book was *My Merry Menagerie* —lighthearted verses and drawings of animals from Alligator to Zebra. *The Mysterious Snippets of Yarn* followed, with a crumbling castle and a curious cast of characters.

In Ireland, Rosemary gave the principal lecture for the Butler Society in the 13th-century round tower of Kilkenny Castle. Her subject was the First Chief Butler of Ireland. She and Charles commissioned a six-foot-high memorial stone, for which she wrote the inscription, to mark the Chief Butler's burial site in County Limerick.

www.ingramcontent.com/pod-product-compliance
Lightning Source LLC
Chambersburg PA
CBHW080148310326
41914CB00090B/894